Claudia Makeyev is an artist and marine scientist. California born, she grew up on both the california coast and the south of France. She currently lives in San Luis Obispo.

She got her art and science education at UC Santa Barbara and graduate degree at The University of Rhode Island.

She writes and illustrates ocean themed kids books. Most recently she completed a book and poster on Yelloweye and Bocaccio Rockfish of Puget Sound for the NAtional MArine Fisheries Service NOAA. She also wrote a sea creature alphabet book for her science education non-profit, The MERMAID ISLANDS CORPORATION.

When not marine biology-ing or creating art she enjoys all manner of ocean frolicking; surfing, sun bathing and beach combing.

For more information on upcoming projects, visit mermaidscientist.com

www.mermaidscientist.com

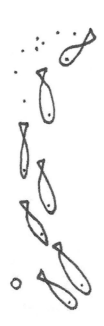

THE

MERMAID MANDALA COLORING BOOK

A MER-MAZING COLOR THERAPY EXPERIENCE

by
CLAUDIA MAKEYEV

For all my truely lovely
friends, family and collegues
who lovingly share my orbit.

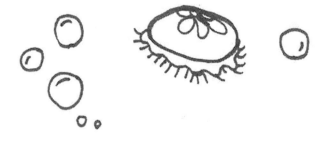

INTRODUCTION

Don't Panic. You are in the right place. In choosing to open this book and take a few relaxing moments for yourself, you made a good decision. The world is loud, rambunctious, and stressful. This coloring book is a quiet escape from the noise of the day. So, get ready to indulge in some much needed color therapy. (colour therapy if not in the U.S.A.).

The traditional Mandala represents an imaginary place that is contemplated during meditation. Coloring relaxing lines, circles and ocean elements let you set sail into your own imaginary place. Within these fun circles and squiggles emerge joyful sea creatures and patterns that are your peaceful sanctuary.

Get yourself a comfy chair or pillow to settle into. A voluminous cushion on the floor next to the coffee table also works. Perhaps sip on some cocoa, tea or even a hot toddy. Try popping those ear buds in, giving everyone the universal sign for "I'm not listening to you."

Now flip through the pages. Pick whichever one inspires you, be it the first page, middle or end. Waves? Otters? Coral? Take your coloring pencils or crayons and settle in for an artsy breath of fresh air.

color, breathe, and enjoy.

May these Anti-Stress designs inspire and relax you.

*Note: This book can be used when an adorable yet fidgety mini mermaid sitting next to you needs a happy distraction on the train, plane, automobile, or restaurant booth. Buy an extra copy to give away for immediate peace and quiet.

Relax

Breathe

Enjoy

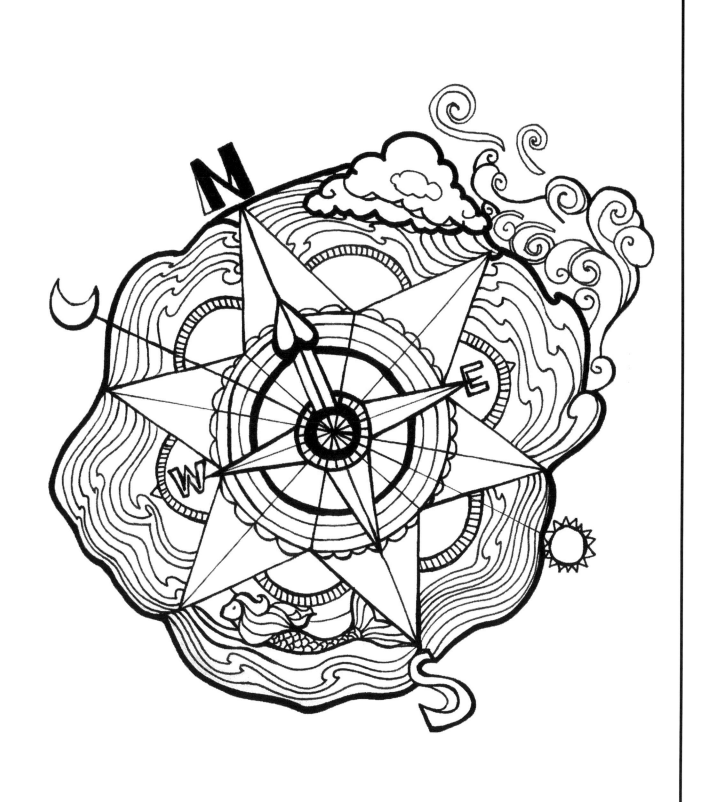

True North

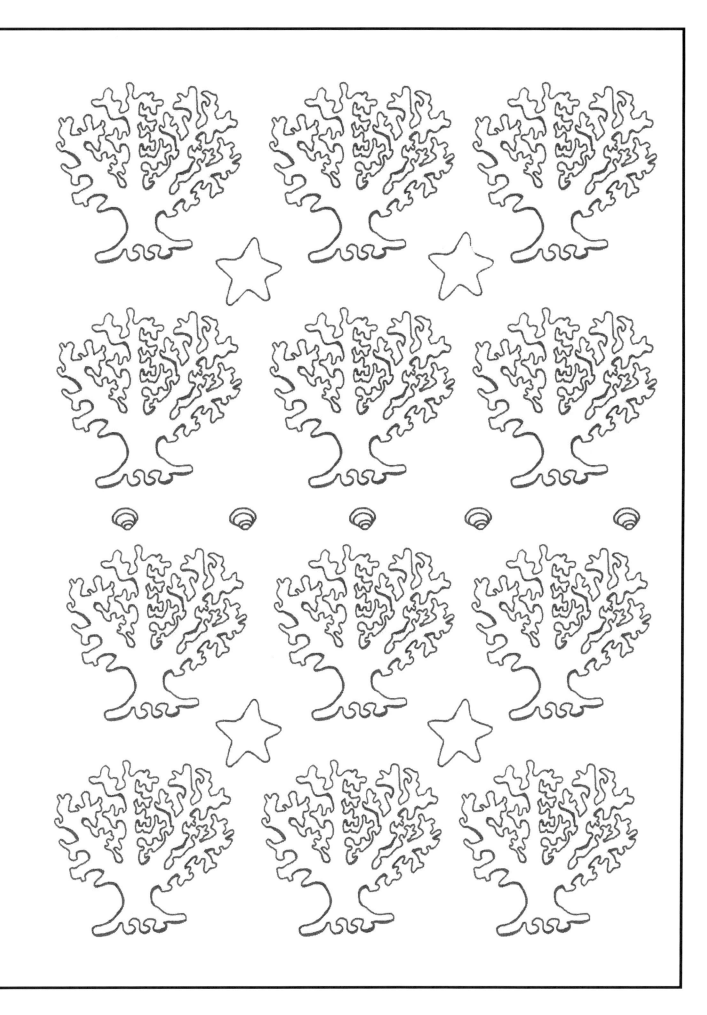

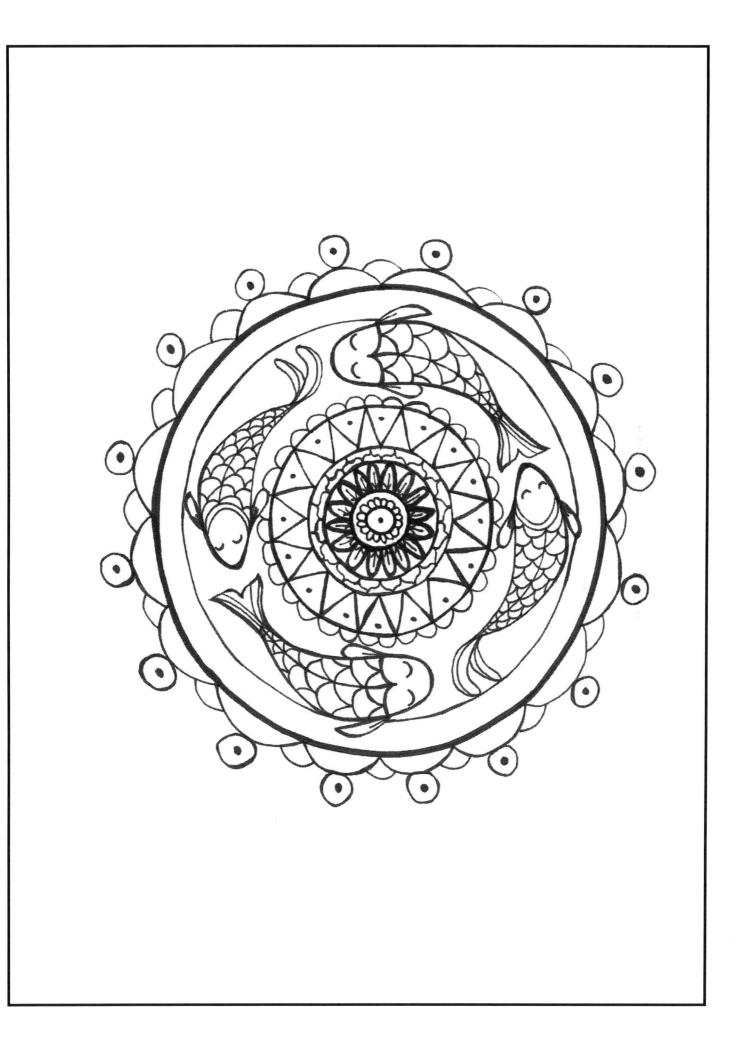

curlew

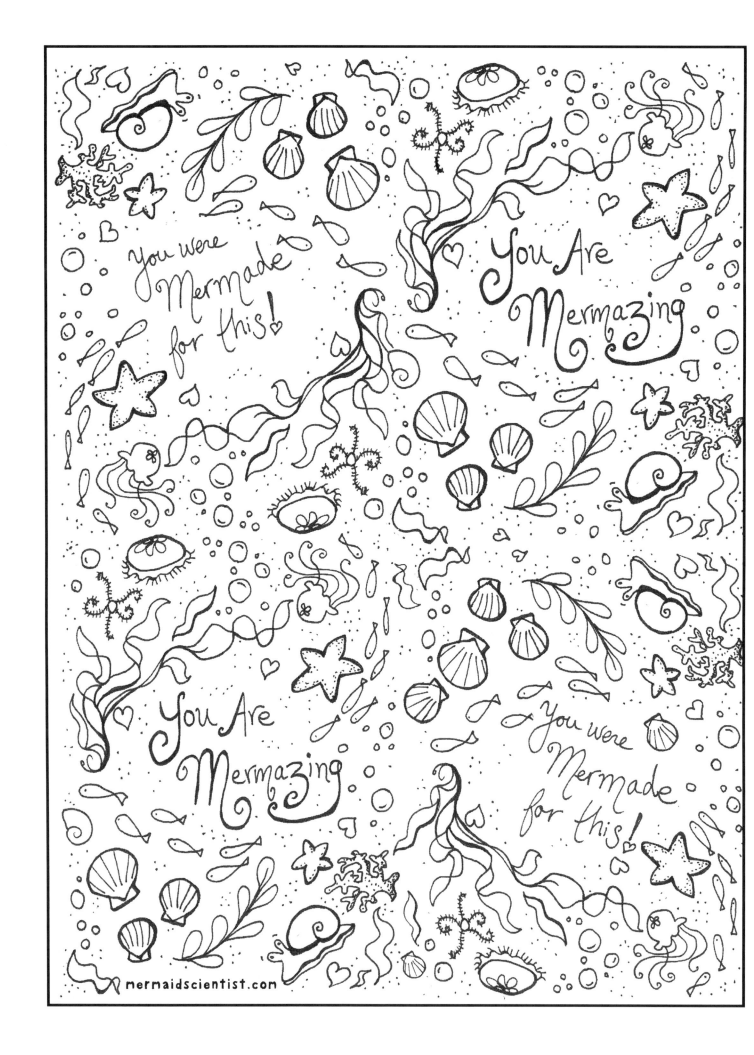

mermaidscientist.com

sea otters

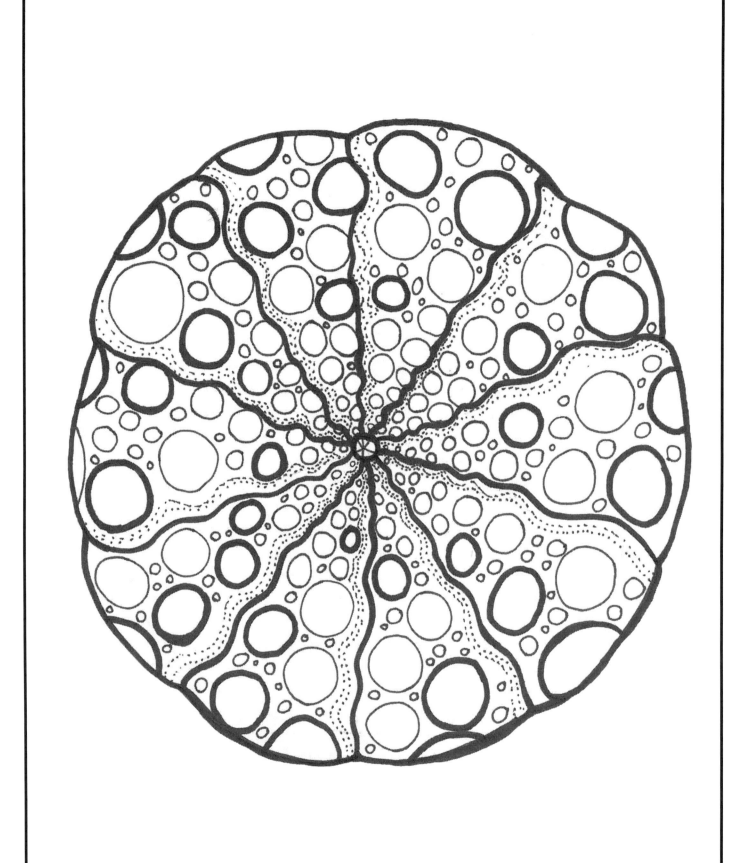

Abalone

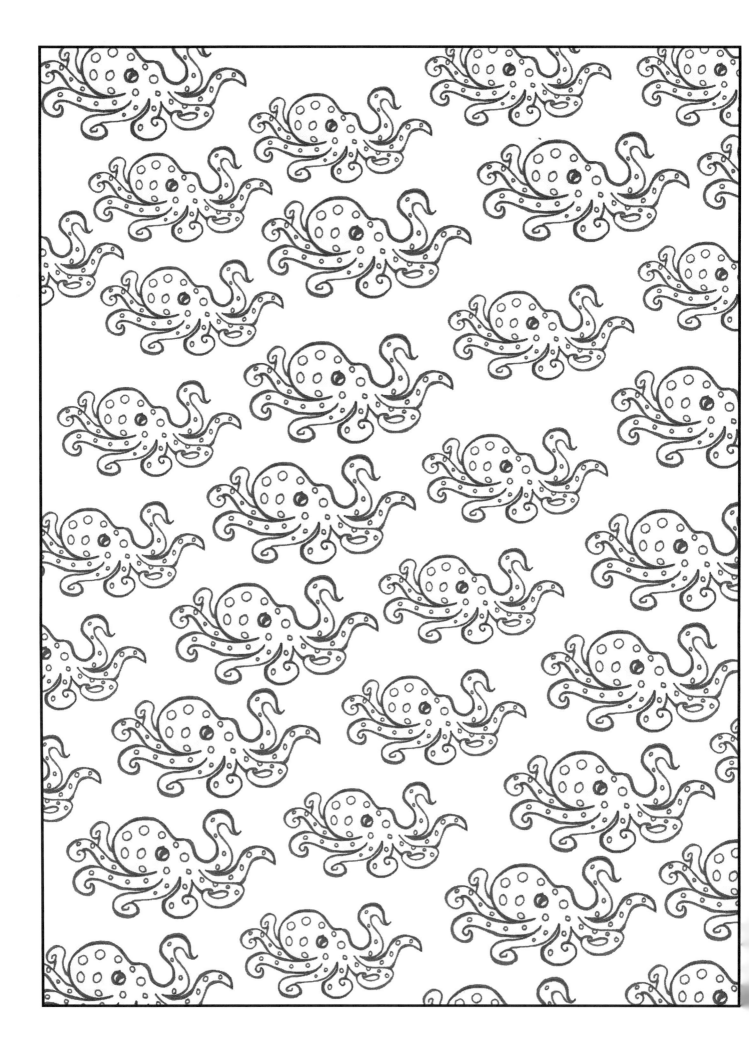

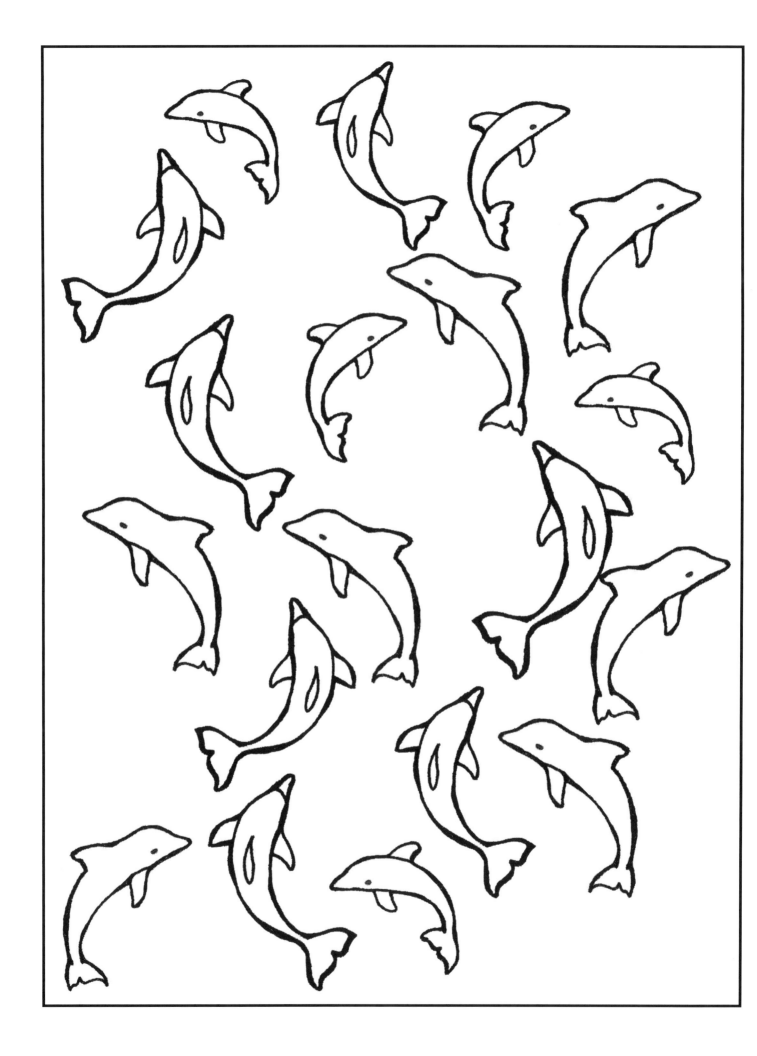

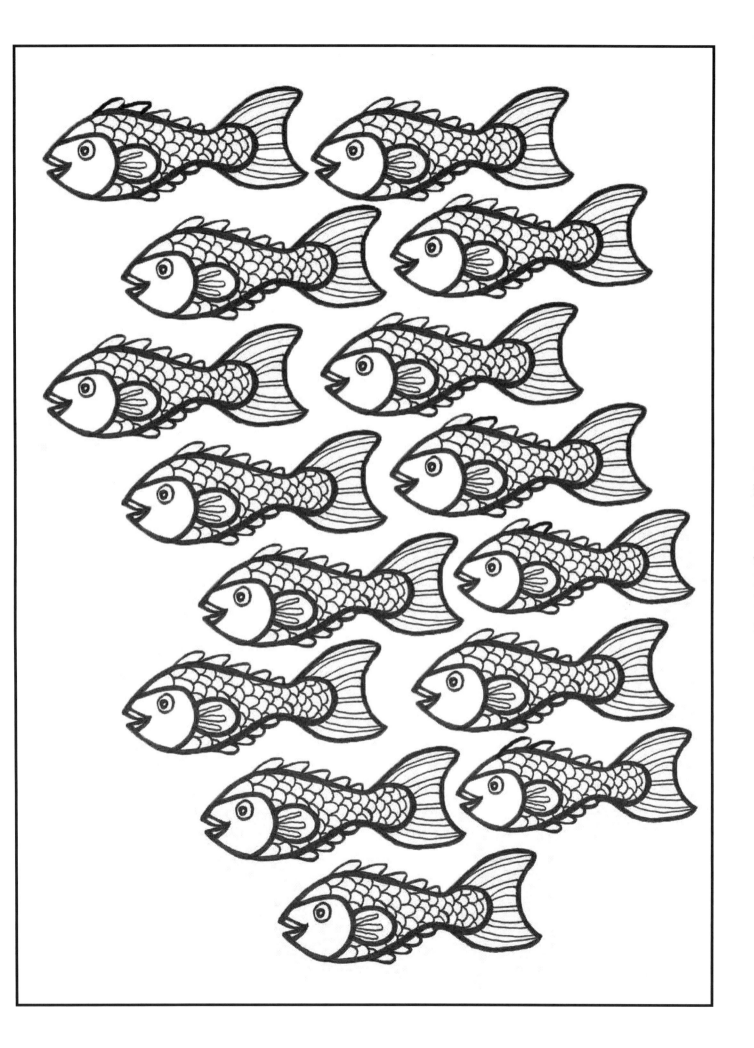

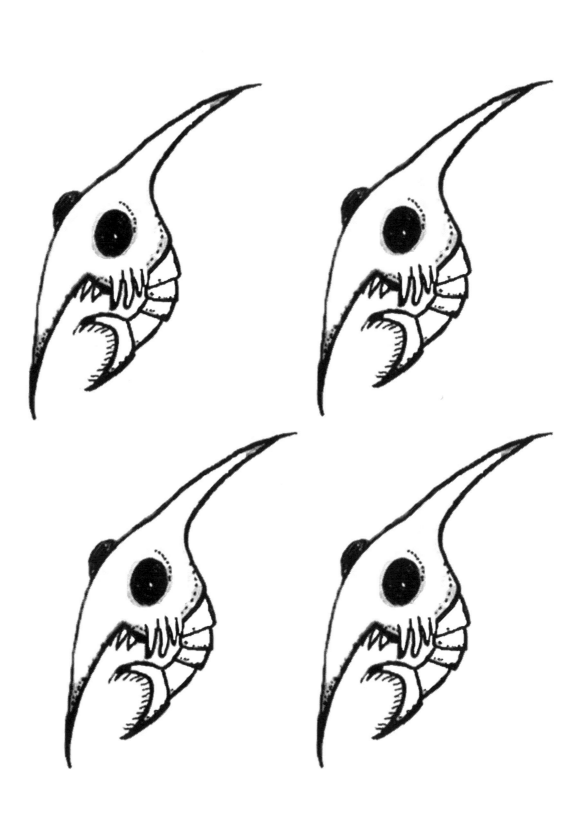

larval crabs

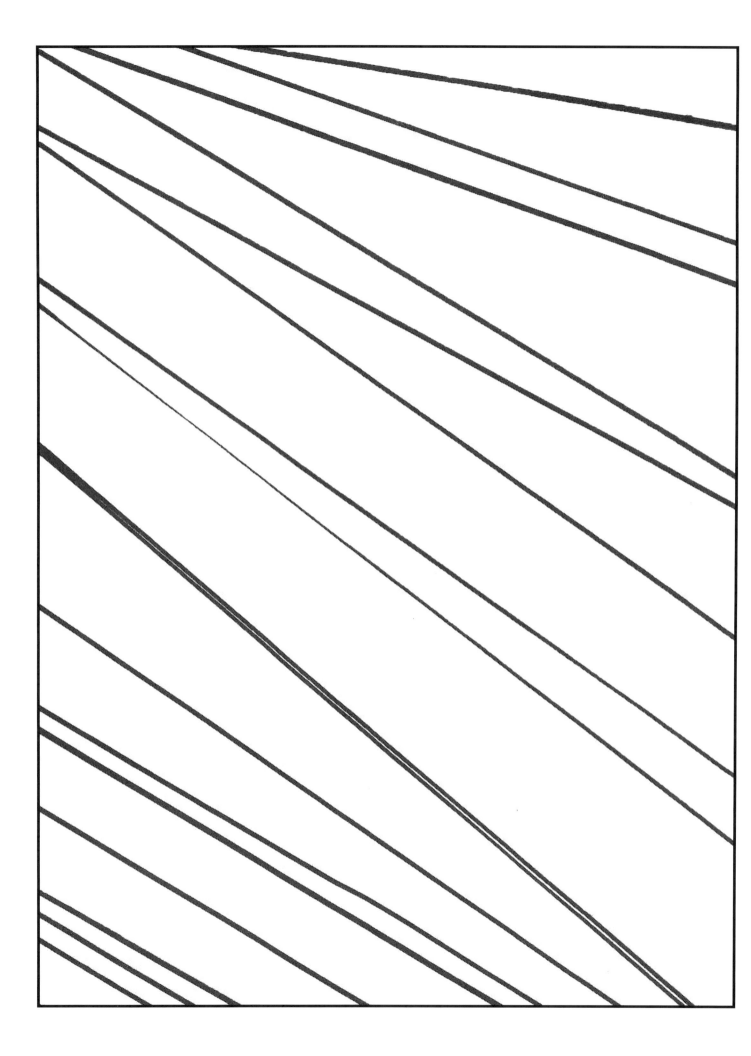

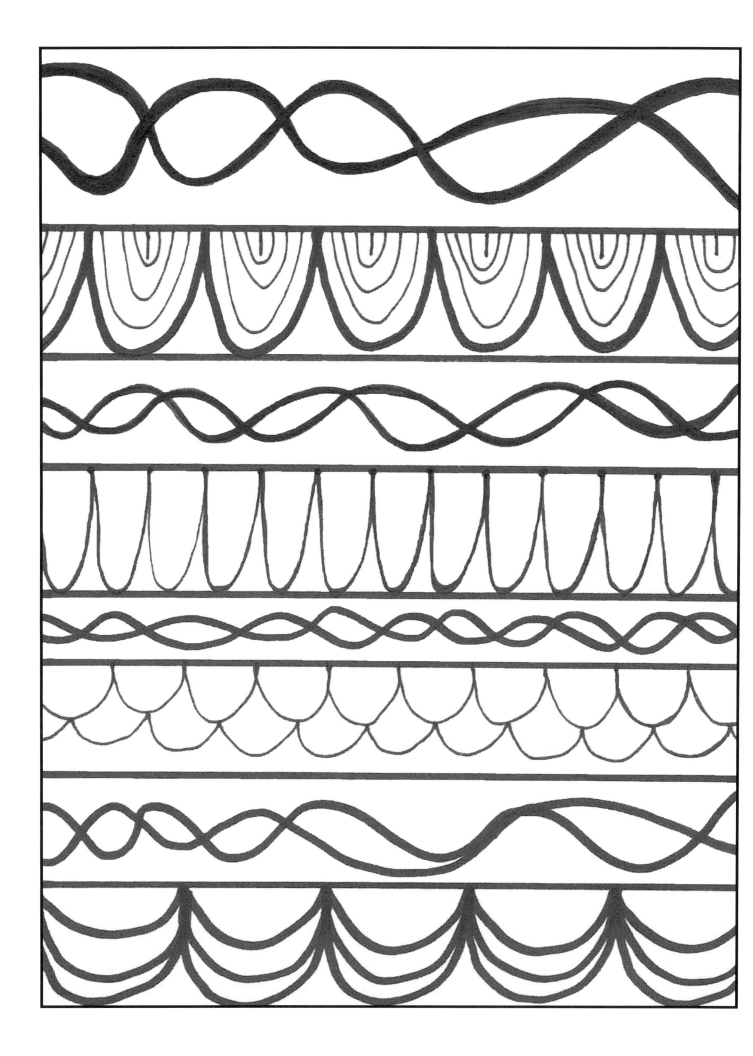

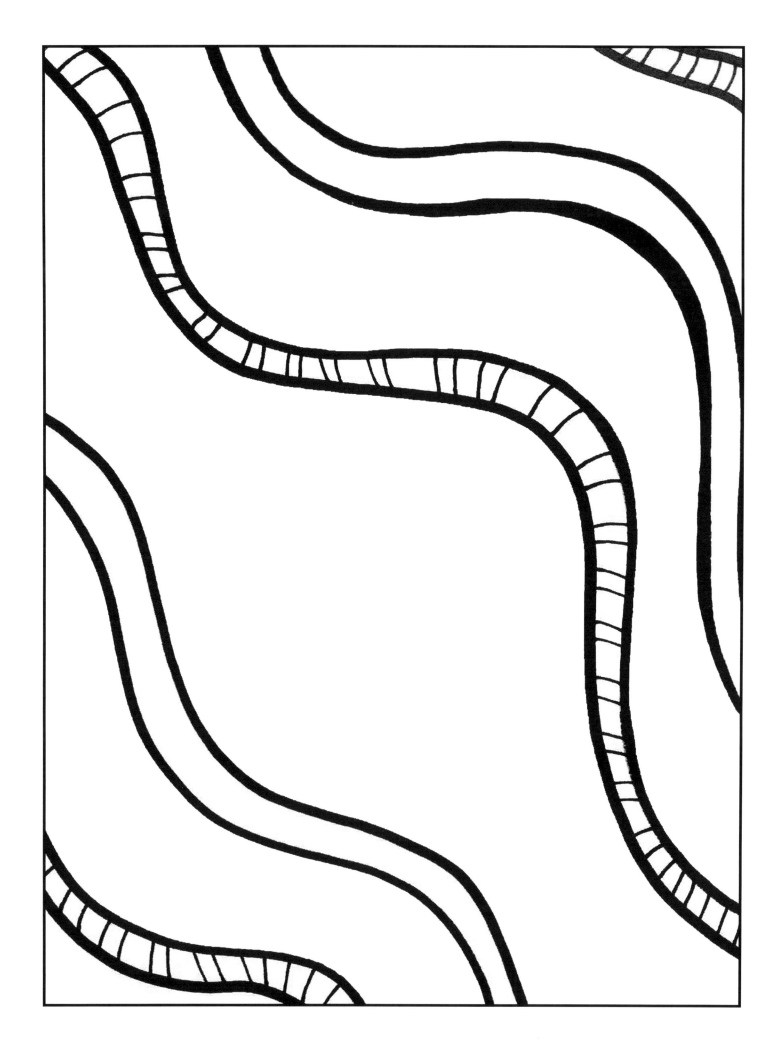

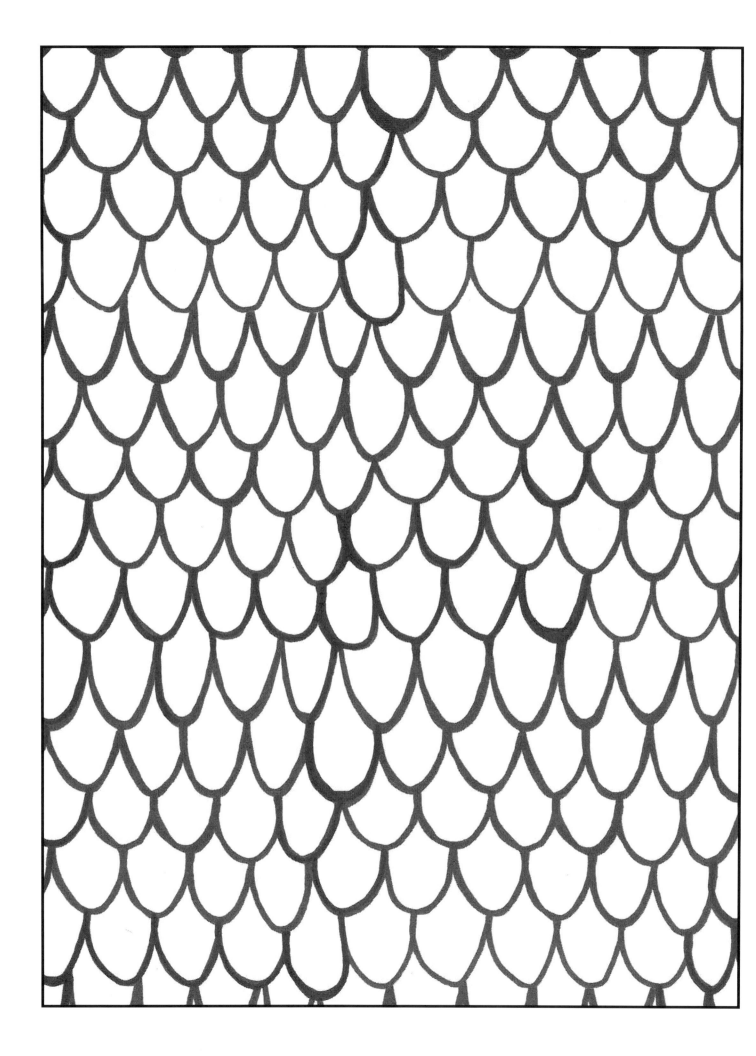

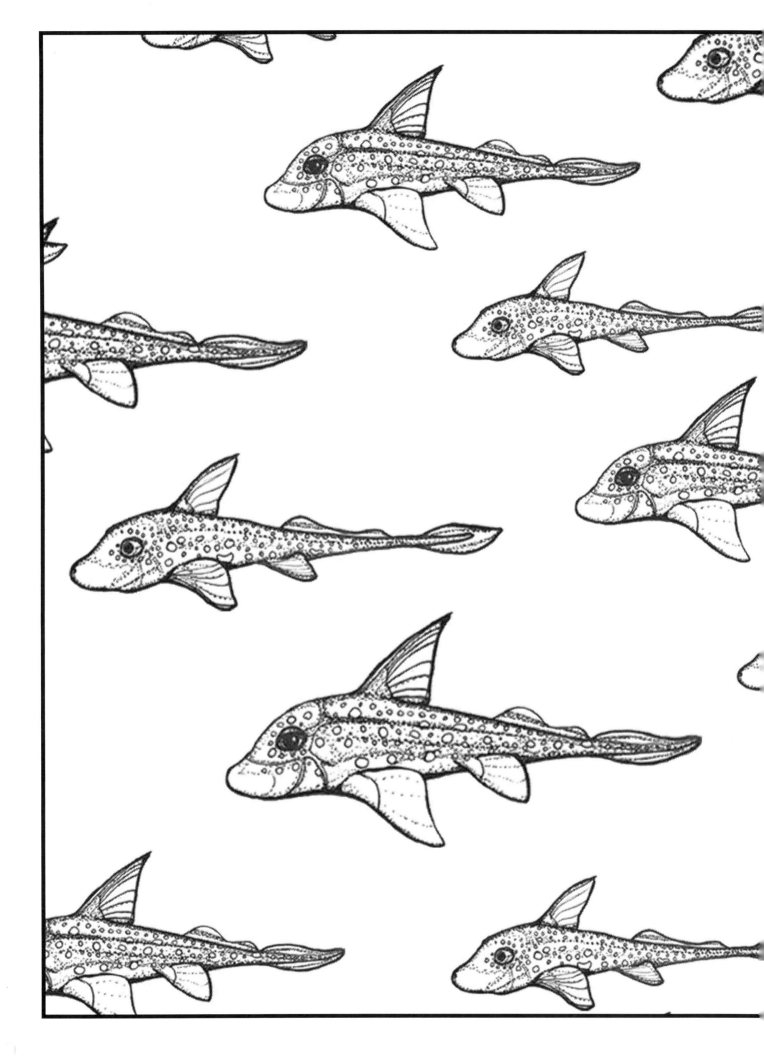

Grateful for the smiles and support
that made for a glorious 2018,

Thank you!

Mom, Ambre and Alex Makeyev, Ken Burgess, Terry Perry, Sheri Perry and Family, my loyal hound Lucy, Teri and Gary Bayus, Aletheia Gooden and Trevor Quirk, courtney Haile, Riki Sesena, Ali Bringham, Jenny Reeves, James Palmer, Michelle Arata, Alex and the whole Hischier family, Brian Robertson, Angela and Peter Ettinger, Sarah Martin, Bobby and Mystica Williams, Sarah McIttrick, James Dalton, Will Harris, Michelle Ruffo and Jeffika, Karin, Satish, Myra and the rest of the motley Montecito crew, Paul connely, Doug Dipple, crystal Weiss, Mermaid Linden, Diane chakos, Kristina "Baku" Webster, Jenn and Ian Kindberg, Alicia De Toro, Ted Thayer and Karin Wells, chad and Kelly Heindrick, Zeke Graff, John Pollock, Jayne Wayne, Missy Reitnercameron, Barnboy, Irene Flores, Kerry Long, Gary, Jeff, Neal Breton and all the artists at The Bunker past and present, Randall and Linda Cox, Kristen Knisely, Michelle Gados, Susie Walby, Elsie Dekawati, Dave Stafford and Neosha Kasheff, Meisha Key, Dan Tonnes, Jen and Jordan Weddel, Rich and Kristen Bell, Perry Rasso, Russ and Sarah Hambleton, Helen Irene, Jackie Lillis and all my Michigan Family, Rockstar Craig Duswalt, Guillaume and Sou Del Motte, Lionel et caro Makeieff, Macha Makeieff et Jerome, Juliette et Manuel, Louise, Arthur, et Felix Deschamps, Daniel, Tristan, Lucy, Anne Marie, and George and all the rest of our Makeieff clan, Angele and Marie and the Lesterps Family, John Ugoretz, Steve Duboyce, John Burke, Lisa Thomas, Gina Smith, Dwight Deakin, Ben Rasnick, Jesse Black, claudia Sotomayor, and all the Tengiri crew; cameron Shepard, Geoff "MIJA", Matt Morey, ol' Drewski, Luke Oliver cromwell, Fearless Izzy, chef Donnie, Tweedle dee and Tweedle dum, Matt Broadhurst, ALL my Ventura surf buddies and Pierpont neighbors that I miss. Kurt and catie Dulka, Greg and John and John and John and the other John and all the other NAVAIR rocket scientists and engineers I had the pleasure of working next to. The San Nicolas Island Black Abalone researchers, Intertidal crew, the Kenners, G. VanBlaricom and the valiant SNI Sea Otter Military Readiness Area Team: Brian Hatfield, Michelle Staedler, Tim Tinker, Joe Tomoleoni, Lilian carswell, Gena Bentall, etc. and other volunteers and researchers that work tirelessly to uncover the biological secrets of San Nicolas Island

(and thank you to all the ones I'm surely forgetting).

COMING SOON:
The Mermaid Science Rockfish Book
created for
the National Marine Fisheries Service

check mermaidscientist.com for release dates

Made in the USA
San Bernardino, CA
24 March 2019